T0004964

Moon Jellyfish Can Barely Swim

Ness Owen lives on Anglesey (Ynys Môn) in Wales where she writes poetry between lecturing and farming. She has been widely published in journals and anthologies including in *Planet Magazine, Mslexia, The Cardiff Review, The Interpreter's House, Ink Sweat & Tears, The Atlanta Review,* and *Poetry Wales.* Her first collection *Mamiaith* (Mother Tongue) was published in 2019. Her poems have been translated into five different languages. Owen has recently taken part in Ù Ơ | SUO, a poetry exchange project between Wales and Vietnam, supported by the British Council. She co-edited *A470: Poems for the Road / Cerddi'r Ffordd,* a bilingual poetry anthology about the infamous road running from the north to the south of Wales.

@ness_owen

Praise for *Mamiaith*:

'Her poems lash with life in language that is both luminous and exhilarating.'
– **Menna Elfyn**

'Ness Owen's poems have an insistent, pent-up energy, gaining friction and purpose from the struggle to be heard – a struggle intensified by the knowledge of silenced voices and silenced language.'
– **Zoë Skoulding**

'Whatever else these poems want from their readers, they certainly refuse to be "wasted on the non-/believer" and the magic of Owen's work lies in how she makes believers of us all—whether we are reading her in Cardiff or in Colorado Springs.'
– **Nina Murray**

'Spare, needle sharp but threaded through with love of country, language, people, past and future, this profoundly political collection stitches us into a rich tapestry.'
– **Kate Foley**

Moon Jellyfish Can Barely Swim

Ness Owen

Parthian, Cardigan SA43 1ED
www.parthianbooks.com
First published in 2023
© Ness Owen 2023
ISBN 978-1-913640-97-2
Editor: Susie Wildsmith
Cover design by Emily Courdelle
Printed and bound by 4edge Limited, UK
Published with the financial support of the Welsh Books Council
British Library Cataloguing in Publication Data
A cataloguing record for this book is available from the British Library
Printed on FSC accredited paper

Moon Jellyfish Can Barely Swim is provided to selected libraries across Wales with
support of The Borzello Trust to promote the reading of contemporary poetry by new
and emerging voices.

I fy ffrindiau pennaf / To my best friends

- Jellyfish are one of the most successful organisms of animal life on the planet. Fossil records tell us that they have been around for more than 500 million years and their morphological characteristics have hardly changed.

- Moon jellyfish aren't strong swimmers and can't resist currents, so they have no choice but to go where the ocean takes them. Their bodies are made of more than 90 per cent water.

- Scientists believe that moon jellies and other jellies thrive in areas that are particularly affected by human activity. Overfishing, ocean warming, and pollution are all factors that reduce moon jellies' predators and competitors and increase their prey. These results provide a more favourable environment for this species. As people continue to increase our ocean activities, the moon jelly may become one of the more successful species in the open ocean.

CONTENTS

Moon Jellyfish Can Barely Swim

5   Put the girl on the shore
6   Message
7   My thirst to know won't end but why should we be the same?
8   Girls of Summer
9   I promise one day I'll teach you how to swim
10   How we glow
11   Get back in the water
12   You can't save everyone
13   Sea Lessons
14   Love song for an uncertain world
15   Birth of a Medusa
16   Conditions
17   Empty Beach Clean
19   Moon Jellyfish Can Barely Swim
20   Gathering Blooms
21   Not Another Sea Poem

Storm Tides

27   *Moroedd Garw*
28   Telling the Bees
29   People would say what a beautiful dress
30   Humming This Tune
32   Blanket Vigil
33   Nain limps through my dreams
35   *Magu Adenydd*
36   The Understanding
37   Disturbing the Artist
38   Five lessons in the art of saying *No*
40   I'm not what happened to me

Captive of the Currents

45 A Failure in Murmuration
46 How to Protest
47 Caernarfon March
48 *Cofiwch*
50 Notes on a *Vowel Hungry* Language
52 Sometimes
53 How She Votes
54 Her Words
55 The Village Formerly Known As

Life in the Water

61 Not knowing how far they were from home
62 Petrichor
64 Slideshow Outside Capel Bach
66 Waiting for Swallows
67 And the goats came
69 Woodchip Decided To Speak
70 For All the Shoulds
72 *Nos Galan Hâf*
74 Jab
76 Ffynnon Gwenfaen
77 Spoor
79 Five Minutes to Spare?
81 Recipe for Cure-All Soup
82 Our Potato Heart
83 Once
85 *Da Bo Chi*

Notes
Acknowledgements
Diolch o galon
I like the idea of poetry bearing witness: An interview with Ness Owen

1

Moon Jellyfish Can Barely Swim

When we see many moon jellyfish stranded in the sand, it is as if we found a bottle with a message inside. We open the bottle, take out the message and read—

Put the girl on the shore

Let her alone with
the currents to the

eager tide's pull of
ebb and gift of flow

to prayers of driftwood
and seaweed notes.

Leave her to the lash of
marram, sting of salt

to the wind-whipped
waves where the

drowned return and
skylines rise and fall.

Leave her side-stroke
out of rip currents, feel

the cold gasp of water
the soft tread of sand.

Let her fall, deep
from dislocation

into the subtle art
of breathing out.

Message

And once
we found
a bottle,
green and
barnacled,
cradled in
bladderwrack
with a paper
rolled inside.
Breath held with saltwater
fingers we delivered it, not to
break the glass hoping for anywhere
far enough, not to be home. The
weight of disappointment shortened
our summer as familiar blends rolled
off our tongues. *Colwyn Bay*. Still a fair
journey but not far enough to ignite
our minds with its *please write back*.

When the ebb tide is lowest the
petrified forest shows. We chased
each other laughing, jumping over
ancient stumps, gaps growing
between us as one of us smashed
it on the rocks and somewhere on
another shoreline not too far from
us, I couldn't help but think of the
man growing old, waiting for an
answer, staring at the same sea.

My thirst to know won't end
but why should we be the same?

Half the day has gone – our words evaporate
into the warm silence of the midday sun. We
listen to the bladderwrack crunch, tiptoe over
beached jellyfish lulled by warm currents.

You want to paddle and have to steady
yourself on my arm. It's easy to forget
your age as our footprints disappear into
the wet sand. Your feet half the size of mine
but I always felt bigger even when I was small.

I fill the silence with stories of beach days
with my friends, how we swam through a
smack of jellyfish but only one of us was stung.
Moon jellyfish glow at night. You don't ask why.

You don't remember these stories or letting
me go out on the bike with no brakes but you
remember the child taken by the wave and the
mother who couldn't lock doors in case one
day her little girl found her way home.

Girls of Summer
(Beaching your critical inner voice)

Summer breathes in
otherworlds.
For a moment I leave her
sand-locked under gull-soar
all hat brim and sighing
knowing she's brought the
wrong shoes. Wasp-waist
pulled tighter for the beach.

Stepping backwards
knees, shoulders, head
underwater, counting
for the ninth wave
muffles her curlew cries.

You never did belong

Salt sting, breath-held
tide carries me further
looking skywards, sun
bursts into depths of blue.

How long, how long
before she drowns
on
the shore?

I promise one day I'll teach you how to swim

It's easy
I tell you,
when I've
no memory
of my feet
learning to
leave the
shore. When
trusting the
water to hold
me up is the
easiest thing
in the world.
How do you
unlearn near
drownings,
life flashing,
calling you
back to the
womb? You
can't fight
your way
through water
muscles must
remember
breathe
think
glide
to swim fast
you must first
swim slow.

How we glow

This is for us
belonging to water
who were warned
not to venture out
of our depths who
ran when flares
sounded to see what
the watch brought back.

Sea butterflies
pulsing through
captives of current
kelp fighters
who scaled the tide-
marked rocks to
find ourselves stranded
catch ourselves falling.

Razor shell collectors
eyes downwards always
looking in the wrong
places, missing the
mermaid purses
finding another
pebble to weigh
down our pockets.

We are braver than
we know. Even in
the smallest light
watch how we glow.

Get back in the water

We'd swum so many times close
to their waiflike glide but always escaped
only when we'd left the water

you found the wrap of lashes
across your legs, smiled, said it only hurt
when you thought about it.

They tell you to get back in
the water. *We wonder why we didn't
get stung.* Pull out the stings

but don't rub. *We wonder if
we are immune.* They tell you least you
have a story to share.

*We wonder why it always
happens to you.* They try to treat your pain
we wonder if we'll be next.

You can't save everyone

They taught me to look
for the darker water, always,
the lack of breaking wave,
unsettling of sand.

Trouble is,
if you keep looking, you
see rips even in the calmest
porth and your fear grows
bigger with every tide.

Soon enough you'll learn
most rips are underwater
never visible from the shore.

Sea Lessons

She tells you everyone
born by sea is brave.

Like the cockle women
you must live by tides,

chasing the ebb, waiting
for the turn. There's little

time between high and
low, but the oystercatcher

knows to swoop at her
chance. She tells you

no one can outrun her,
only count for the ninth

wave that'll carry you to
shore. Like the marram

grass weavers, bend, fold
over and under from

mother to daughter pass
on all that you learn.

Love song for an uncertain world

My mission in life is not merely
to survive, but to thrive;
– Maya Angelou

So here we are unlikely
miracles washed in waders'
tune, barefoot on faltering
strandlines, combing
through

the spiral-wrack moments
          that call us home:

the anemone opening
          to water,

the periwinkle clinging
          to gullied stone,

               the sea pink lullabies,
          sky-burst of lapwing,
                    lichen-kissed rock.

Birth of a Medusa

*Jellyfish have a polyp phase when they are
attached to coastal reefs, and a medusa phase,
when they float among the plankton.*

Do you remember
        the moment?
                Moon aligned, ocean calling

shocked into being

        so ill-fitted for
            the water

                and yet here you are

          graceful drifter

free to float

        light drawn
            sensing safety is

             a bloom of your own.

Conditions

When environmental conditions
are conducive, polyps give
rise to medusae.

Weren't you given the sea?
Bewildering waves
echoes to sit between
arms flayed in a dance
with gravity and this
endless calling.

// change stage / change colour /
change diet / change shape /
change name / change place //

Isn't life full of fades
and surges and this
waiting for the right
conditions?
The temperature drops
winter settles
this is your cue.

Empty Beach Clean

This year we only
find left-footed shoes.
We wonder where all
the right ones have gone
and how we'd walk
without them. The
slower we move the
more we discover
sifting through
plastic ruins, freeing
bladderwrack from
the choke of net.

We find a piece shaped
like Bridget's cross
underneath some quartz
stones. A sign, you say
and tuck it in your pocket.
Following the trail of
shore-crab moults, we
reach washed-up goat
willow, roots already
darkening. One branch
shows life in leaves and
catkin. A gentle tap
and they'd carried up-
shore like snowflakes
hoping for ground.

The sea wind brushes
the sky with grey.
They'd promised rain
and there's comfort in
the uncertainty of sky,
the fall of thunder-drops
and the sweet smell of
summer's rain.

Moon Jellyfish Can Barely Swim

Imagine the weight of
that secret when you live
amongst the swimmers
shrinking to survive,

the flow pushing you
further, the gulls mock
moon confides with
sun, and you meeting
the ceaseless ebb and
flow of want.

Waiting for that one
current to take you,
and leave you aground.

The faintest imprint,
memories on sand.

Gathering Blooms

Of all the potential mishaps that
can cause a nuclear plant shutdown,
from an earthquake to operator error,
the one that you might least expect is
a swarm of jellyfish

What do they see?

A simple creature, drifter, survivor
daring to imagine power is in connection,
a shared intention, collective luminescence.

Good ideas will always be battles
but wisdom is in the struggle,
no one starts a revolution alone.

Change starts at the fringes,
instinctive gatherings, places
where hope begins to grow.

The first step is believing
even the smallest creature
can change the world.

Not Another Sea Poem

This poem won't tell
you that in this life, there's
no more of a sure thing
than tide-turn as faithful
to you as the rise and fall
of sun. It won't boast that
lunar days are longer,
talk of saltwater, teach
you to sink or float.
It won't worry you with
sea levels, storm surges,
oceans taking up heat,
the glaciers' retreat.
If you are away from it
you won't curl up and dry.
It won't taunt you with slack
tides or haunt you with
waves that come unannounced.
It won't bring you back presents
of fractured greed. Between
these lines you won't hear the
breaking wave scream *stop
dumping your shit in the sea.*

2

Storm Tides

Eat the storms, Mother said
– Damien Donnelly

Moroedd Garw

From here, you see the storm
coming the sky presses on you
and clouds gather strength.
Gafael yn dynn, gafael yn dynn.

Rain comes and you
lose direction, watching for
the white wave that carries
back the drowned.

Catch
the cold gasp calling,
invite
the unravelling into water.

Reach out your arms,
lean back,
scream at the stars,
and remember,

this day you learnt to float.

Telling the Bees

Tonight we'll search the sky
for Caer Gwydion, Arianrhod's

pathway to heaven and for the
brightest of seven sister stars.

The bottom of the garden
feels a galaxy away as we tread,

weightless, in white suits and
whisper to honeyed hives

mae 'di mynd, turning them
half-circle, away from the sun.

People would say what a beautiful dress

They tell us we shouldn't
speak of the dead but
Netty's frock called me

from the bottom tallboy
drawer, tucked tightly
in the corner, unfinished.

A defiant red, though I only
knew her in black and white
and from other people's

stories. Putting on her dress
I found her shape, the curve
of hips that loved to dance.

It clung to me in a spark
of charges. Mam always
said she'd finish the un-

done hem, so one of us
could wear it and Netty's
frock could tell another story.

Humming This Tune

When I remember you,
I remember us in that photo
of a summer visit. Standing
by your front door, back to
back, three months between us.
Almost women, so alike and so
likely to be the black sheep.

(*Oh our mothers cried*)

You're holding the kitten as wild as you.
I'm growing our family fear (but I
keep that secret well). I wear the
blue wedge sandals which looked so
much lower in the catalogue, but
I still got to keep because we never
send things back. We make do.

After this we'll walk, follow
our noses, sing, mess with lyrics
(*Come on Eileen, Paid â dangos dy din*),
until you, always wanting to get away,
take the shortcut through the marsh path
knowing, in new shoes, I won't follow
but neither of us would ever give in.

We're walking in different directions
firing song lines over gorse and hawthorn
(cos *we are far too young and clever*).
When you arrive back alone, panic rises,

searches begin and I wander further
in honeysuckle lanes, summer-dizzy in my
new shoes still singing, not looking behind.

When they find me your eyes are pools
glistening. You promise you'll never
leave me again. I bought a tree for you
but I can't unpot it and I said I wouldn't
write poems about you but where else
can I find you but in photos of summer
and humming this tune when I know
you won't follow.

Blanket Vigil

Blanket-wrapped
he sits at the side
of my bed. It's far
past midnight

and we haven't
slept. We listen to
classics on the radio
suck boiled sweets to

stop my dry throat.
I'm too old for his
white horses to send
me to sleep but I'm

too young to give up.
You have to find a
way, he says, to stop
living alone in your

own head. The gap in
the curtains lets the
moonlight slip down
the wall till it dips under

the horizon and together
we wait for first light.

Nain limps through my dreams

After Lan Anh

Nain limps after
            falling from the bus
                        on the way back from town.

Coesau   *araf*   *pen-glin*   *stiff*

Cold cream cheeked, hair roller set,
warm crooked hands, smelling salt pursed,
whisky rescued breath, sister by her side,
salt-air burns, soft rain teases, foghorn sounds
in seasons of low clouds, side winds, spring tides
waiting for the seas to meet, bus stop bound.

(she can't run sees the barn owl
gallops home to check we're all alive.)

Limping Nain
              goes to town

Town quietens
shops shut, chapels closed, factory finished
Janglo, mwydro, hel clecs, rwdlan, malu awyr
Town says yeah, town says no
Bechod, cwilydd, mynadd
Hush, hush, hush
(Quietness is what we do best)

Town listens
town blames, town doesn't like what she sees,
town is afraid, town is angry, town loses her tongue,
town gives up.

Limping Nain
                    goes to town

She won't wear a bra
her feet hurt
she wants to change
her shoes.

I hold her name.

Magu Adenydd

What is it about flight?
Weren't we born treading

air searching for ground
so why this longing

between our shoulders
for the hushed, unfolding
of feather?

Bodies sprout wings or
they don't. It's in our
genetics.

Sometimes we fall
to earth. Sometimes
someone will catch us.

The Understanding

Paul Spider's house looks
over my house, I know

he's watching. Pity shadows
behind nicotined curtains.

A solitary witness
to my ritual existence.

He told me one drunken
New Year's Night by the

dying poinsettia in the
kitchen but my house

overlooks Paul Spider's
house. I've seen his

computer-fascination.
I told him one drunken

New Year's Night. I think
we have an understanding.

Disturbing the Artist

After watching some of the painting of 'The Hall of Illusion'
by Edward Povey

You have been warned
Don't talk to the artist

don't ask him where to
begin or the names of

those soldiers, you know
never saw home again.

Linger here
behind him, hungry

for any story that isn't
yours. Search for the

agony in faces you know
will betray your form.

Who isn't drawn to fire?

you ask the heartbeat
in your womb. Pour

your life over his shoulder
knowing he won't look back.

Five lessons in the art of saying *No*

Lesson 1

Hands over our faces
spying through a trickle
of light between our
fingers, we watched
other mouths for the
nasal *n* the rounded *o*.
Our silenced tongues
pressed ready in the
roof of mouths.

Lesson 2

We wrote letters in
the air, drew the hill
and curve in sand,
held the sounds in
other mother tongues
repeating them over
till they soared from
our stifled throats.
Na, nee, kāo, hayir.

Lesson 3

We practiced on each
other. An assertive smile
a *not now, I'll get back
to you later*. The words

found a comfortable
home in our mouths.
We stood up, stilled
our bodies, interrupted
and held our ground.

Lesson 4

We ventured to the
streets in groups of
three. Urging each
other to speak louder
to programme our
default to *no* before
we said *yes*. We set
our priorities. Looked
upwards to our goals.

Lesson 5

Back in the classroom
teacher had left us
a note on the board:
I'm thankful for this
opportunity, but need
to pass on it right now.
Please read out loud:
No is my choice.
I have to mean it.

(No, I can't teach you that.)

I'm not what happened to me

Who said a story isn't a story until you can look backwards and see
the blistering trail left behind?

They tell me skin remembers tear, bone remembers break,
heart remembers sting, blood responds to call.

Healing starts near the edges and grows to fill the void.

The future is the moss-cracked path, the ivy-choked wall,
five riotous sparrows dust bathing on the road.

An alabaster sky promising nothing to a watery sun.

3

Captive of the Currents

Relax, stay calm and float

A Failure in Murmuration
(Ynys Môn Votes Blue)

Two days before voting
three hundred starlings
fell from the sky on
an unnamed road
by Llyn Llywenan
at the fall of dusk.

It was easy to blame
farmers first then gases
seeping from Wylfa,
deep in her half-life
sleep or the shock
wave of a jet fighter.

As the island-sky turned
a shallow-blue thoughts
focused on a falcon, a
predator causing sudden
change of direction.
A failure in murmuration.

Panicked bodies colliding
purple, blue and tear-shaped
golds but what is three
hundred in a quarrelsome
flock of thousands? Nature
is cruel, there's no escaping.

Birds at the end of the flock
fly too close to the ground.

How to Protest

After Paul Davies

Sometimes the bravest
thing is to hold your
oppression above your
head like a trophy
burnt with letters
already branded
on your tongue.

Standing this still
holding the weight
takes practice but
what then, when
the audience has
gone and you're left
with nothing more
than hardwood
seasoned to last?

Weaken the fibres
with the curved edge
of a reshaped blade,
in rocking motion
we'll carve love
spoons from
their Welsh Nots.

Caernarfon March

We arrived later than
we thought, running
to catch up, me and
an old school friend
shortcutted through
the car park like we'd
lost the bus. *Holyhead
Welsh* standing on the
verge, watching clouds
breaking over Môn,
looking down Balaclafa
Road to a sea of red,
green, white, of yes,
of Cymru, of *rhydd,
fy ngwlad, fy nyfodol.*
A wave flowing from
Doc, rushing through
arches built to keep us
out, sunglasses on for
face detectors. *Ti ddim
yn ffycin cael fy wyneb.*
By Black Boy, clickers
count our true numbers.
The castle is surrounded.
Stones echo with our soft
tread onto Y Maes, no
tears of blood, today.
Our hearts in the hands
of each other.

Cofiwch

Remember it said
bold white letters
painted onto the

Faenol stone next
to *Free Wales Army*
and *All shall be well.*

Remember it said on
journeys south before
radios and seatbelts

when we sang 'Be-Bop-
a-Lula' and 'Calon Lân'.
Remember it said when

I asked questions and
believed the answer
because they could.

Remember it said a
whole village drowned
which caused no ripple

to friends who knew of
girls stolen by fairies,
a woman crafted of

flowers and a giant that
walked across seas. In
dreams I saw our village

drowned and watched the
last beckoning hands
vanish beneath the water.

How would I forget?

Notes on a *Vowel Hungry* Language

After Natalie Scenters-Zapico
With found quotes about the Welsh language

What is language more

than a window to a world,

a lullaby to ear, a scissors to

cut, vibration stuck in throat?

An open or shut door and you

are where you find yourself.

On the outside still hearing

your grandmother's prayers

protecting, living in the space

of her absence or chasing words

that demand more with their peaks

and dips, shouting of all the mistakes

you've ever made. How many times

must I say that names matter?

An ugly pointless language.

It's foreign to me

native gibberish.

A maypole around which

hotheads can get all nationalistic.

Energy spent, no distance covered

appalling and moribund

cat-walking-across-the-keyboard

like someone trying to get phlegm out

of the back of their throat.

A danger to life on the roads,

a weapon inflicting hatred, misery

& disinvestment.

A political tool that harms children.

That words grow into worlds if

only you'd let them. Tonight,

I'll sit watching the setting of a

stubborn sun, raise a glass and

switch from one language to another.

A language no one else really

needs or wants.

I love the Welsh language, but all those

consonants together can be so intimidating.

Sometimes

For RS

Sometimes there are places
we must go to touch the

edge of the water, see
our fractured reflection,

understand that silence
is more than a gagged

mouth, a wooden Not.
Silence is the weight of

water when we fight for
air, and graffiti is our voice

to shout. *This is our story.*
Chapters are waiting.

Over-paint us as you will
brushstrokes will not erase

us. Walls are held together by
the weight of well-chosen stone.

How She Votes

She walks, runs,
drives to the polling
station, patiently
waits for her turn,

hears the cell door
slam, feels the pain
of hunger, the choke
of feeding tube, the

sting of a slapped cheek,
smells vomit in her hair.
Marks her cross, folds the
paper, catching the shape

of her shadow on the
ballot box, marches
away knowing strength
lies in the linking of arms.

Her Words

Like precious stones
she kept them hidden
safe from those
they might offend,
away from those who

would replace them for
words that slipped
easy off their tongues.
Alone she tasted
sweetness, sang them to

every bird or creature that
would listen but not answer
like they were borrowed
not given, for her to shout
from mountains, what a gift

to know your land
through language, to hold
the words that will always
belong. At night she feared
the day she'd not remember,

she whispered them
into the mirror, waiting for
forgetting as it tiptoed
nearer. Knowing, without
her words, she too was lost.

The Village Formerly Known As

Between the last lime-washed
homes, red valerian still grows
through stone, surrendering to

a summer that has long begun.
Bold-bricked chapel peeks
through her painted gates

side glances an *I told you so*
to the empty cottage cluster
following the curve of shore

and they try to hold back the
waves with armours of stone
as the dunes shrink back into

themselves in a hum of
dwindling names and we
are in love with ghosts.

Where can we swim
without jellyfish? they ask.
The sea wind wails *Going, going—*

4

Life in the Water

Life can only be understood backwards;
but it must be lived forwards.
– Søren Kierkegaard

Not knowing how far they were from home

And after the third
day the sun lulled
the wild bees awake.
I left my desk to follow
one – dandelion, daisy
to apple blossom.

Her, alone as me in this
March sky so peacefully
blue, waiting for the
hum of others on
days where our
earth stands still.

Mae'r byd 'di newid
I'm close enough to
whisper, to tell her
of my daughter
undefended in the
hospital caring.

A worker like her
circling further,
home imprinted.
Everything must be
for the hive. First
days will always
be the worst.

Petrichor

One day you'll
thank the leaves

for turning, praise
the mountains for

warning though
there's little chance
our paths will change.

You'll thank the
fat rain-beads

falling, the earth
scent, freeing

herself from stone
and the Weather

Gods that will
find you alone.

You'll thank the
roots for halting,

the seeds for
waiting and the

orchestra of
scents that will
point the way.

One day you'll
thank the air for

lifting, the echo
leaving and the

morning after
when you learnt
to love the rain.

Slideshow Outside Capel Bach

You're Sunday School boy
by my side on the bench in
the slide of new polish
swinging our legs.

We're bursting to be freed
to chase under thorny trees
but you're faster than me
and I can't catch you up.

You're lead man and
I'm curtain girl.
The crowd always loves
you, I wait for cues.

You're fairground boy and
we ride the rollercoasters.
You grip my arm, scream
more than I do.

You're city boy, move far
away, don't come home,
live fast, love fast,
reject me on Facebook.

You're prodigal boy
come home sick and grey.
I see you on the shore
but we only wave.

You're bus stop boy
I'm always running late.
I pass you, tell myself
I'll pick you up later.

I'm outside the
chapel and they're
playing your tune.

Bus-stop-prodigal-city
-fairground-lead-man-
Sunday-School-boy.

I don't go in.

Waiting for Swallows

Sky watching, we already
know they're late. We
reassure each other with
storm tales, swoops blown
off course, March brought
the heat too soon, April
held onto the snow.
We begin to look in old
nests, like mothers of the
disappeared our world
grows smaller, forked
tales haunt the corners
of our eyes. We mistake
swift dives, the flick of
a wagtail for our own,
tilt our heads to listen for
the pulse of their wings
the drill of their song.
We wake one morning
to see eight on a wire.
Still giddy with relief
we're too late to notice
they aren't arriving
they're gathering and
they don't stay.

And the goats came

Down from Gogarth
leaving their mountain
like they'd always been
waiting to taste the
privet poison and take
back what was theirs.

And then peacocks in
High Street, Bangor,
MPs and second-home
owners, they started
travelling in the dark
and this man got a
warning for driving
to walk his dog.

And *You Must Stay
at Home* drones
in Neath Port Talbot
like these alien spiders
for the people not
listening and the ones
that don't watch the
news and even the
Senedd made rules
just for us.

And everything feels
like a long time and
the weather is ... and

a phone call always
breaks up the day
and there's repeats
on the telly and I'm
getting these emails
how to look after your
mental health and I'll
be honest, I haven't
opened them yet.

Woodchip Decided To Speak

Can't you see
the splendour in
my devotion?

The satisfaction
of ripped corners.

Your delight in
my demise won't
bring it closer.

I am ingrained

You will breathe
my dust. My name
will trip on your
tongue.

I will destroy
these walls,
take plaster
with me.

This is my house.

Are you ready
for my fall?

For All the Shoulds

We were far too
young when we met.

(Should)

Maybe I liked your
company a little
too much.

(Should be)

Perhaps I thought
things would get
better if you stayed.

(Should be going)

Maybe I hoped
both of us
would change.

(Should be doing)

Perhaps I used you
to punish others.

(Should be ashamed)

Maybe you were
my perfect excuse.

(Should know better)

If I add an of
you're no more than
a common mistake.

(Should ~~of~~)

You did not happen.
Take away the sh
and you are helpless.

                    (~~Sh~~ould)

You can't be sounded
out but you never were
phonetic, were you?

Nos Galan Hâf

Last night, at 21:42, someone took
a chainsaw to the osprey nest

It was a Friday night
last of the month
under a paling pink
moon, winter still

standing in blackthorn
waiting for the fight he
wouldn't win, when
unseen by the

camera's persistent eye,
a chainsaw snarled
36 seconds from felling
cut to fall. 20% of the

population in one clear
strike. *Just didn't make*
sense to rid us of our nest-
faithful birds. An act as

random as a road scheme
that ploughs through
ancient oak, as *violent*
as a holiday village that

fells a squirrel's drey.
As *deliberate* as a
conversion that destroys
a swallow's nest.

Perhaps April was the
cruellest month but it's
still early spring. Their
inbuilt clock ticks on.

Jab

The hospital queue is almost a
school reunion. In the haze of
familiar chaos, I stumble backwards
to morning break, summer of '83,
sun leaking through corridor windows

as we queue alphabetically two
by two outside matron's office,
in the scent of Limara and M block
toilets. My surname ties me to Terry
who laughs at my Howard Jones

folder, tells me I've hands like a
Nain Goni. I study my fingers
and his, trace the tidemarks on
his school shirt. Up close, he's
shorter than me and it's hard to

see why his voice sparks fear in
the hallways. Back in line, there's
talk of fishhook needles that rip skin
like it was paper. Before we reach
the door, Terry turns to the rest,

tells them his skin will break any
needle. We shuffle in, sleeves rolled
up, needles already waiting. I turn my
head as Terry hits the floor. The nurses
whisper *how the mighty have fallen.*

They take us to another room, ask
me to sit with him until he feels
better. Fiddling with my friendship
bracelet, I mumble how boring our
lesson was this morning. *Gis a gweld*,

he reaches for my arm, fitting his thumb
and forefinger around my wrist bone,
tells me, we're friends now. *Friends
don't tell each other's secrets.* No one
asks what happened when we leave

the room and Terry dead-arms the
boy at the front of the queue, tells
him pain stops pain like he'd done
him a favour, then side-kicks the fire
door, lets me through and elbows

his way to the lunch hall. I watch
him disappear into a blur of bottle
green and wish him friends like
mine and someone at home waiting,
that would sit and listen to this story.

The Covid queue creeps
on, broken into gaps of social
distance and I look backwards
down the growing line hoping
for the boom of a voice to echo.

Ffynnon Gwenfaen
(Gwenfaen's Well)

Full oft have I repaired to drink that spring,
Waters which cure diseases of the soul
As well as body! And which always prove
The only remedy for want of sense.
– Lewis Morris

It was so easy to give up in the
summer scorch of grass, imagining it
wasn't our time to find this place, to
offer two stones to cure us of what is
woven beneath our skin. Only then

did Borthwen make sense –why quartz
is so easy to find on her glinting sands.
We held the milky stones warm in our
palms, roaming headland until we found
her lichen-rich cell and bubbling spring,

journeying cliff-wards back to the sea.
Waters littered with jilted gems. As
we swung our arms our fists began to
close not wishing to add to Gwenfaen's
troubled hoard. We held our beach diamonds

sunwards to let the light shine through, put
them in our pockets and carried them home.

Spoor

Woman accidentally joins search party looking for herself.

They took us to the last
spot sighted, to find any
traces she'd left behind.
Trick was to remain silent,
to remember the importance
of looking ahead and low,
sideward glances.

We watched for broken
spider webs, ghost scales
and leaf depressions,
followed trampled blades
of grass that whispered of
direction, paid attention
to absence.

We studied the description:
Female approximately middle-
aged, average height, normal
weight. Last seen eating a
sugar-free cereal bar, checking
her phone and looking into the
distance. Shoe size unknown.

Before dark, they found footprints
believed to be a woman's.
There was something so familiar
about the stride we couldn't help
but measure our paces alongside

heelstrike-footflat-midstance-pushoff

One of us stepped inside and
it fitted like the glass slipper.
I think it's me she mouthed into
shadows as they told us all women
take smaller steps except when they're
fleeing and actions can be taken to avoid
being tracked by imagining the tracker
and eliminating your own traces.

Five Minutes to Spare?

You could:
Knock out a few emails
make a smoothie
hit a punch bag
say your prayers.

Drink a bottle of water
make a phone call
read a few pages
tell someone
that you care.

Slow down
catch your breath
walk to meet a friend.
300 beats of your heart
570 steps.

Think of the season
(She was just five minutes from home)
make adjustments
(just five minutes from home)
nights are closing in.

Keep alert
keep to the well-lit
keep your house keys
in your hand.
(five-minutes-from-home)

Walk with purpose
head up, eyes front
wear something
suitable on your feet.
Remember you are only
five minutes from home.

Recipe for Cure-All Soup

Gather the ingredients
lying at the bottom
of your fridge
awaiting resurrection.

*You must use
what you have.*

No need to measure,
add what's growing
in your *cynefin*.

Stir with intention –
ladle in a love poem,
just for this moment
listen to it bubble,
rest amongst steam
vapours as they curl
into air.

Taste with eyes shut.

Our Potato Heart

This year we grew a potato heart –
lifted it from the earth with gentle
cupped hands. Displayed it on the
kitchen table, took photos,
posted, got likes.

But what would we do with a potato
heart? Who would dare harm it
with peeler or knife? We hid
it away from the sun, to rest
and grow a thicker skin.

Even in darkness it began to sprout
so we waited for season turn, to
return it to the ground, wondering
what we'd do if we grew
a new heart each year.

Once

The Spotted Rock-rose is a locally rare species.
The flowers are pale yellow with a dark crimson
spot at the base of each petal. It flowers only once
during its lifetime and sheds its vivid petals within
hours of doing so.

After all these years we had
such little hope of finding
this brief life. Waking early
from dark, crimson-spotted

dreams, wishing our days
passed until the flowering
season. Counting our months
in daffodil, violet, sea pink

and the fortunate ones
who flower summer long.
We measured our steps
in red-flushed leaves,

ranged wind-cut heath,
inched over rocks born
of fire, wondered if we
really believed in ghost

flowers who thrived
in this bareness. It took
a stranger to point out
what was beneath our

feet, us seaworn and
salt-blinded. We
knelt to meet her
wilful yellowness,

surrendered one ragged
petal at a time. We
promised we would
return each year.

Da Bo Chi
(Voyager 1)

Our words wander with you
endlessly through the cosmos
iaith y nefoedd, interstellar
leaving our heliosphere.

Particles zip and stream, as
you'll splutter into silence,
growing colder, further from

us, the smallest blue speck
in a magnificent beam
of scattered light.

Notes

The jellyfish quotations at the front of the book are from 'Sea Wonder: Moon Jelly' (marineesanctuary.org, 2020), 'Corals and other Invertebrates: Moon Jelly' (oceana.org, 2020) and an article written by Josep-Maria Gili, Ainara Ballesteros & Macarena Marambio 'Birth of a Jellyfish: Why Blooms are on the increase in the Mediterranean' (oceangraphicmagazine.com, 2022).

You can't save everyone:
Porth – Bay (Welsh).

The Right Conditions: The epigraph is from the journal article 'Indoles induce metamorphosis in a broad diversity of jellyfish, but not in a crown jelly (Coronatae)' by R. R. Helm and C.W. Dunn (https://doi.org/10.1371/journal.pone.0188601, 2017).

Lovesong to an uncertain world: The quotation is from 'Maya Angelou: In her own words' (bbc.co.uk, 2014).

Birth of a Medusa: The epigraph is from Janet Grieve's article 'Open ocean – Larger plankton in the food chain' (TeAra.govt.nz, 2006).

Gathering Blooms: The epigraph is from Patrick J Kiger's article 'Jellyfish Invasion Shuts Down Nuclear Reactor' (nationgeographic.com, 2013).

Moroedd Garw:
Moroedd Garw – Rough seas (Welsh).
Gafael yn dynn – Hold tight (Welsh).

Telling the Bees:
Mae 'di mynd– She's gone (Welsh).

Humming this Tune:
Paid â dangos dy din – Don't show your arse (Welsh).

Nain limps through my dreams:
Coesau araf pen-glin stiff – Slow legs stiff knee.
Janglo, mwydro, hel clecs, rwdlan, malu awyr – Jangling, moidering,
carrying tales, talking rubbish.
Bechod, cwilydd, mynadd – Pity, shame, patience (Welsh).

***Magu Adenydd*:**
Magu Adenydd – Literally to grow wings – but also means to leave home
(Welsh).

I'm not what happened to me: *I'm not what happened to me; I am what I
choose to become* is an alleged quote by Carl Gustav Jung.

How to Protest: After Paul Davies' 'Welsh Not to Love Spoon' exhibition.

***Cofiwch*:**
Cofiwch – Remember (Welsh).

Notes on a *Vowel Hungry* Language: After Natalie Scenters-Zapico's poem
'Notes on My Present: A Contrapuntal' with statements by President
Donald Trump in *Poetry* (December, 2018).

Life in the Water: Quote taken from Adam Phillips' 'Philosopher of the
Heart: The Restless Life of Søren Kierkegaard by Clare Carlisle' article
(guardian.com, 2019).

Not knowing how far they were from home:
Mae'r byd 'di newid – The world has changed (Welsh).

Jab:
Nain Goni – Insulting name for an old woman (Welsh slang).
Gis a gweld – Let me see (Welsh slang).

Ffynnon Gwenfaen: Extract from the poem 'The Sacred Well of Gwenfaen, Rhoscolyn' by Lewis Morris.

Cerddinen:
Cerddinen – Rowan (Welsh).

Recipe for Cure All Soup:
Cynefin – Difficult to translate. The place where you come from or the place where you belong (Welsh).

Once: The epigraph was taken from *Anglesey, Flowering Plants and their Habitat* by Gareth Rowlands (Cambrian, 2018).

Da Bo Chi:
Da Bo Chi – Goodbye (Welsh).
Voyager 1 has been travelling through our solar system since 1977 and is now right at the edge of it with its batteries running out. It carries a golden record with information about Earth and humanity, which includes a greeting in Welsh in case it encounters alien life.

Acknowledgements

Many thanks to the editors of the following publications where versions of some of these poems have appeared:

Black Bough Journal, Culture Matters, Eat the Storms Journal, Ink Sweat & Tears, New Welsh Reader, Planet Magazine, Red Poets, Seventh Quarry Journal, Symposeum Journal, The Cardiff Review, The Interpreter's House, The Lampeter Review, Shortest Day, Longest Night (Arachne Press, 2016), *Noon* (Arachne Press, 2018), *Time and Tide* (Arachne Press, 2019), *Tymes Goe By Turnes* (Arachne Press, 2020), *Pandemic Poetry Anthology* (Gloucester Poetry Festival Press, 2020).

'Telling the Bees' was Pushcart nominated in 2020.

Thanks to Damien Donnelly for permission to quote from his collection *Eat the Storms* (Hedgehog Poetry Press, 2020).

Some of the poems were born in workshops including those attended through *Poetry Wales* and The Cheltenham Poetry Festival.

Diolch o galon

Warm thanks to Susie Wildsmith for her kind support and inspiring editing and to everyone at Parthian.

Much love and gratitude as always to family and friends here and passed who have carried me through calm and rough seas and to the village of storytellers that raised me.

More thanks to all my poetry friends who have supported me especially all the people at The Ucheldre Lit Soc, Rhwng, Cybi poets and the community that is @TopTweetTuesday.

To the 3 Gs and C – *werth y byd i gyd yn grwn*.

I like the idea of poetry bearing witness:
An interview with Ness Owen

Ness Owen lives on Ynys Môn (Anglesey) in Wales where she writes poetry between lecturing and farming. She is the winner of the Greenpeace Poems for the Planet competition 2023 and her writing has been widely published in journals and anthologies including *Planet Magazine*, *Mslexia*, *The Cardiff Review*, *The Interpreter's House*, *Ink Sweat & Tears*, *The Atlanta Review*, and *Poetry Wales*. Her first collection *Mamiaith* (Mother Tongue) was published in 2019. Her poems have been translated into five different languages. Owen has recently taken part in Ù Ơ | SUO, a poetry exchange project between Wales and Vietnam, supported by the British Council. She co-edited *A470: Poems for the Road / Cerddi'r Ffordd*, a bilingual poetry anthology about the infamous road running from the north to the south of Wales.

Rooted in her island home, Ness Owen's second collection explores what it is to subsist with whatever the tides bring, in poems that journey from family to politics, womanhood and language.

Moon jellyfish live a life adrift, relying on the current to take them where they need to go. They are the ultimate survivors and one of the most successful organisms of animal life. So how do they thrive in the open ocean when they can barely swim?

In the ebb and flow of an ever-changing world, starlings fall from the sky, votes are cast, a village is drowned, a petrified forest is revealed and messages wash up in seaworn bottles on the shoreline, waiting for answers that will not come.

'This collection has me wanting to tug at people's sleeves, to share extracts, to say 'Look at this!', 'Listen!' It's a book of word-wonders, memorable to the last. It has head and heart, and wisdom (yes, that). There is a keen care for preciousness under threat, where the Welsh language is imperilled, just like the natural world's rich diversity.' – **Fiona Owen**, *The High Window*

'Throughout the collection, the poet takes risks, relishes collisions and uneasy contrasts. She keeps the reader on their toes, but seeks to treat them as confidante and friend. There really is something to excite every taste because the poet has such skill and technical grasp of form and phraseology. The writing feels fresh, inclusive and wise, a really lovely blend of the good things that poetry can bring to the intellect and to the senses.' – **Pat Edwards**, *London Grip*

What book is currently on your bedside table?
I actually don't read in bed as it would probably mean that I wouldn't be able to put the book down easily and go to sleep so my ever growing reading pile is beside my favourite armchair. The three books at the top are Kathleen Jamie's *Sightlines* (which I'm reading very slowly as it's such a beautifully haunting read and I like to have a gap between chapters), Jan Morris' *In My Mind's Eye,* and I'm re-reading New Zealand poet Ankh Spice's extraordinary collection *The Water Engine*. I've also just finished Gwyn Parry's evocative collection of stories *Y Gwyn Braf.*

Where and how do you write?
Like many poets, I often write in my head and have a huge collection of notebooks of different sizes so I can carry them with me. I have to write notes down quickly or I generally forget them and what sounded like a wonderful line is gone. Once I have an idea that is bursting to be on the page, I write a full draft in a larger notebook then onto the computer in my little office; usually with the quiet company of my dog and the cats and, if the Ynys Môn (Anglesey) sidewinds permit, the windows open. When I'm editing, I try and walk my poems as it helps me with the rhythm and line breaks. I'm lucky enough to have access to fields and

shorelines where I can read out the lines to myself and not bump into many people!

What inspires you to write?
There is a long list of things that inspire me: reading other works, language, place, injustices current and past to name a few. I sometimes write to remember or to try to understand. I like the idea of poetry bearing witness, poetry as a protest and in our present climate emergency there's always something that needs writing about. Meeting with poetry friends in local groups and going to workshops also inspires me greatly.

Where did the title *Moon Jellyfish Can Barely Swim* come from?
Growing up by the sea, I've always been fascinated by jellyfish. In my childhood memories, they are part of the scenery whether it was a solitary passer-by or beached blooms covering part of the shore. They are the ultimate survivor although they are powerless in currents and go where the sea takes them but they have also shut down more than a few nuclear power plants across the world. Like many other species, they are affected by the warmer seas, pollution, overfishing and over-tourism. In their case, the warmer seas appear to be increasing the frequency of larger blooms.

Where are your favourite places to go to think?
Living on Ynys Môn (Anglesey), I feel spoilt for choice for beaches, wetlands and spaces where I feel there is more sky than land. I'm especially fond of the shores of Porth Dafarch and Aberffraw but I also love our little mountain, Mynydd Twr, and Penrhos woodland. Walking is a big part of my writing process and I like to wander, follow my nose and go where the path takes me. I'm a very slow walker as I often stop to look at things so I'm usually better off just taking Nansi my dog who doesn't seem to mind the pace.

Ness Owen, Spring 2023

PARTHIAN *Poetry*

The language of bees
Rae Howells
ISBN 978-1-913640-69-9
£9 | Paperback

'Rae Howells forges a unique and sparkling language, which is capable of giving us all the wonder and richness, the multi sensual onslaught, of the world around us.'
– Jonathan Edwards

How can we have hope in a world that is dying? With a forensic eye, Howells takes us on a journey through ordinary human lives and the extraordinary natural world we are in danger of losing.

Strange Animals
Emily Vanderploeg
ISBN 978-1-913640-70-5
£9 | Paperback

'A beautifully crafted rumination on identity, ancestry, and the environments that make us who we are.'
– Isobel Roach, *Wales Arts Review*

A Canadian grandchild of Dutch and Hungarian immigrants, Emily Vandeploeg explores issues of language, ritual, death and identity.

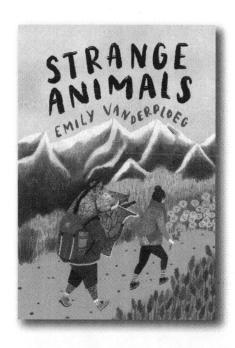

PARTHIAN *Poetry*

Hymnal
Julia Bell
ISBN 978-1-914595-11-0
£10 | Paperback

'Moving, tender writing with a haunting evocation of place and time.'
– Hannah Lowe

Visiting Aberaeron in the 1960s, Bell's father heard a voice directing him to minister to the Welsh. This unique memoir in verse tells a story of religion, sexuality, and family.

Pearl and Bone
Mari Ellis Dunning
ISBN 978-1-913640-72-9
£9 | Paperback

'These polyphonous poems are voices at a protest march, strong in their oneness, furiously, exhaustedly casting their spells and blessings.'
– Ellora Sutton, *Mslexia*

Beautiful, emotional and richly imagistic, Mari Ellis Dunning presents mothers in many forms: those experienced, chosen, unwitting, and presumed, asking us to consider the true nuances of motherhood – delicate as pearl, durable as bone.

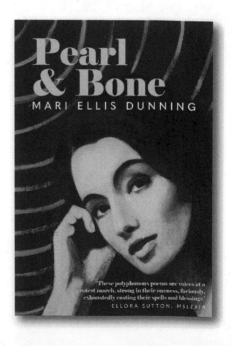